North Walsham
& District

A Second Selection

'Bruff' Hewitt and Dan Mount at the old town pump, *c.* 1910.

BRITAIN IN OLD PHOTOGRAPHS

North Walsham
& District

A Second Selection

Neil R. Storey

The
History
Press

First published in 1998 by Sutton Publishing

Reprinted in 2012 by
The History Press
The Mill, Brimscombe Port,
Stroud, Gloucestershire, GL5 2QG
www.thehistorypress.co.uk

Half-title page photograph: The 12.23 p.m.
Sheringham to London Liverpool Street
Express approaching North Walsham, *c.* 1930.
Title page photograph: Delivery man for J.B.
Craske's fishmongers, *c.* 1930.

British Library Cataloguing in Publication Data
A catalogue record for this book is available from the
British Library.

ISBN 978-0-7509-8900-1

Typeset in 10/12 Perpetua.
Typesetting and origination by
Sutton Publishing Limited.
Printed and bound by CPI Group (UK) Ltd,
Croydon, CR0 4YY

Little changes! We are all used to water collecting under the railway bridge on Norwich Road after heavy rain. Think of how it must have been when there were two bridges serving the two stations. Quite a crowd is gathering here to watch as vehicles plough through the flood; the car in the foreground, pulling Peruzzis' ice cream cart, is finding it heavy going after severe rainfall, *c.* 1937.

CONTENTS

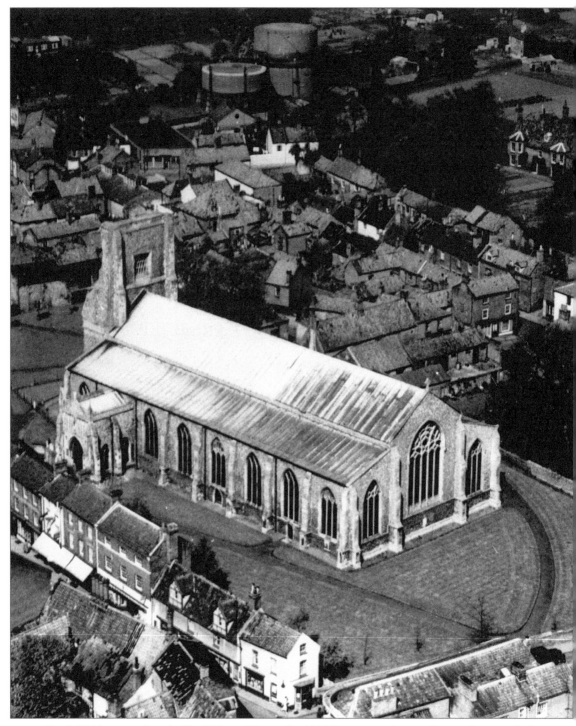

North Walsham was described by William White in his 1845 Directory as ' . . . a pleasant, but irregularly built Market Town. . . . It consists chiefly of three streets, forming an irregular triangle . . .' This magnificent aerial study of St Nicholas' Parish Church, the Market Place and Vicarage Street area, taken roughly 100 years later, proves that, at this time, little had changed from when White described it.

INTRODUCTION

The first volume of photographs of North Walsham and district was published in 1995. In this second selection, I have been able to focus more on areas of the town and district changed almost beyond recall or, in some cases, lost forever. Thanks to the photographers, professional and amateur, at least images of these streets, shops, people, places and events have been recorded for posterity. However, one cannot help but wonder what the town must have looked like before the advent of popular topographical photography. From the time of the Norman Conquest the arable land surrounding the town was divided into three fields – Southfield, Millfield and Northfield. Each field was cut into strips bounded by balks or low grass ridges while the outlying lands provided rough grazing for cattle and wild pigs.

The town itself grew outwards from the Market Place, with its distinctive narrow shops built on the thin circling strip of chartered ground around the parish church where the original wooden market stalls were erected. Most of the houses at the time were also made of wood, with roofs of thatched reeds provided by the plentiful reed beds in the marshy districts close by. Just about all of North Walsham, with the notable exception of the parish church, was burnt to the ground in the space of about two hours on 25 June 1600. The fire, which began in the house of 'a poor and lewd character' named Dowle, caused £20,000 of damage, a veritable fortune in those days. The town that was reconstructed after the fire remained structurally similar until the middle of this century. William White in his directory of 1845 described North Walsham as ' . . . a pleasant, but irregularly built Market Town, on an eminance, with a declivity descending northward to the river Ant. . . . It consists chiefly of three streets, forming an irregular triangle, intersected by a few cross lanes.'

Law and order was maintained from 1846 at the Theatre Street police station, complete with two cells, under Superintendent Thomas Boutell and two constables who did their best to 'keep the peace'. Petty Sessions were held at The King's Arms every Thursday with Judge Thomas Jacob Birch presiding, George Wilkinson, Clerk, and James Dye, Bailiff. There was a town workhouse,

A very fine multi-view postcard from North Walsham, *c.* 1904.

built in 1786 off Mundesley Road at a cost of £1,100, but after the town joined the Erpingham Union paupers were removed to houses of industry at Gimingham and Sheringham while the old Walsham workhouse was let to Mr Fidell Deman, who established in it a processor's of Norfolk-grown flax employing about fifty local men, boys and girls.

The market then, as ever, was held on a Thursday; in those days, however, it seldom commenced before 2 p.m. in winter and 6 p.m. in summer. There was also a Corn Hall, built in 1848 in the yard of The White Lion by J.H. Reeve and a number of £10 shareholders for £900. (When it was no longer used for trading it became a popular venue for dancing and public events. However, it was demolished in the 1960s to make way for the Bank Loke car park.) The annual fair for horses and lean cattle was held on the eve and day of the Ascension (Holy Thursday) with hiring sessions for servants on two Thursdays before and one after Michaelmas.

By the turn of this century the town remained one of the important market towns of the county. It was served by the Great Eastern Railway (GER) from Liverpool Street in London and so connected with the south and west of England; and by the Midland and Great Northern (M&GN) to Yorkshire and Scotland. The wealth of the town and the surrounding district was founded upon agriculture, as ever, with both the arable and livestock markets. Its prosperity was further endorsed by a wide variety of innovative local industries ranging from the manufacture of all manner of agricultural machinery and implements, such as those made by Randell's Foundry, to the exceptional works of Cornish & Gaymer, ecclesiastical carvers. In 1912 the town's businesses comprised a very different compilation of shops and trade to those familiar to us today. It had 8 outfitters, 14 bars and pubs, 8 butchers, 5 bakers, 3 blacksmiths, 4 fishmongers, 3 wheelwrights, 3 clock and watchmakers and 3 saddlers, along with a kaleidoscope of old trades such as a leather seller, pianoforte tuner, reed thatcher, billposter, mole destroyer and only one estate agent!

The twentieth century has seen some of the most dramatic and sweeping changes to the way we all live, work and enjoy ourselves around North Walsham and district. One 1920s guide stated ' . . . it is possible to walk mile on mile o'er heath and holt, through wood, through brake and only here and there have need to touch the highway at all'. Today the town is expanding all the time; maybe now more than ever, as we approach the millennium, we should look to the past and what is left of it before we are so quick to forge on into the future.

Keep yew orl a'troshin!

The Market Place is closed and a policeman on duty at the entrance barrier to the festivities in honour of the coronation of King George V, 22 June 1911.

CHAPTER ONE

AROUND THE TOWN

Norwich Road, c. 1905. This important 'entrance road' to the town was made up from a 'rutted and pot-holed lane' to form the final section of the Norwich to North Walsham Turnpike, and opened in 1797. However, it was well over 100 years later that it was improved again to have a proper road surface and footpaths.

The 4.55 p.m. London & North Eastern Railway (LNER) Sunday Service train from Cromer to London Liverpool Street pulling into North Walsham 'Main' station (note the roof of the booking hall to the right), *c.* 1935. The express journey from North Walsham to Liverpool Street in London took about three hours.

North Walsham 'Main' station, *c.* 1914. This was the town's first railway link, proposed by Lord Suffield in 1863 with initial finance promised by the GER. The line, constructed by Lucas Brothers, was completed from Norwich to the town in 1874 with the extension to Cromer following in 1877. Tragically most of the station buildings were demolished in early 1998.

The 12.50 p.m. Cromer to London Liverpool Street train and its carriages line the entire length of North Walsham 'Main' station, *c.* 1935. The number of carriages required reflects the popularity that this service enjoyed for so many years. The engine itself stands beyond the end of the platform with the goods yard to the right, much of which was rented by Barclay Pallett & Co. Ltd for the distribution of their cattle feed and coal.

A derailed train on the crossover at the Cromer end of North Walsham 'Main' station, *c.* 1910. Such a mishap would have caused considerable problems on the line until suitable winching equipment arrived to lift the engine back on to the rails.

M&GN Railway, North Walsham 'Main' station staff, *c.* 1941.

A goods train leaves the M&GN 'Town' station to cross the second railway bridge, about 250 yards from the GER station, over Norwich Road, *c.* 1930.

A busy day at the 'Town' station, *c.* 1930. This was North Walsham's second station, opened in 1881. The line, proposed in 1875 by Sir Edmund Lacon, the Yarmouth brewer, began as the Yarmouth and North Norfolk Railway running from Yarmouth to Stalham. Local businessmen Messrs Ezra Cornish, of Cornish & Gaymer, Randell and Cubitt financed the link to North Walsham.

After a short dispute with the East Norfolk Railway the new railway line connected with the Lynn & Fakenham Railway, thus enabling a rail run up to Leicester. The line was later taken over by the M&GN. In the late 1950s and early 1960s passenger services were axed on much of the M&GN, the final nails knocked in by the Beeching Acts. Pictured is the 'Town's' last day of passenger service on 28 February 1959.

'Don't say petrol – say Pratt's' reads the sign on the side of the wonderful old petrol truck in front of Starling's Garage on Norwich Road. Pictured shortly after John Starling acquired the garage from Frank Mann in the late 1920s, the business not only carried out vehicle maintenance but dealt in motor and pedal cycles as well as running the first taxi service in the town. In 1933 the business was purchased by Stuart Harmer and Bill Scott, and the 'garage by the station', by whose large forecourt clock everyone set their watches, traded as Harmer & Scott until 1984, when it was bought out. The premises has retained its links with things of a vehicular nature though; it now deals as a tyre and exhaust centre.

Cattle being driven down Grammar School Road, c. 1925. Once such herds were familiar sights, filling the roads and lanes around the town on market day. After sale at the Yarmouth Road livestock market they would often be driven down Grammar School Road to the waiting cattle trucks at the M&GN station.

Calf show at the Yarmouth Road livestock market, *c.* 1947. This area was originally owned by The Cross Keys Inn and was renowned for the cock fights held there. In the 1880s fairs and shows were forbidden in the Market Place and the inn's land was acquired for the sale of livestock. The cattle were herded into small groups in the Market Place and adjoining streets to await their turn to be sold. Many of them were even taken by rail to cities in the Midlands, where Norfolk beef was held in high regard.

Yarmouth Road, pictured with its dusty unmetalled surface and leafy green banks in the early 1920s. This section of the road is lit by a single gas lamp. The entire town was lit in those days by about thirty lamps. The town council had a curious arrangement whereby street lamps were not lit for five nights at the time of full moon – provided that the moon came out! Criticism from the council would be directed at the town surveyor if lamps were lit when the moon was out, and conversely if lamps were not alight when the moon was clouded over.

North Walsham police station and court house, *c.* 1910. In those days Petty Session hearings for the Tunstead and Happing Division were held in the court house every alternate Tuesday. Many local dignitaries sat on the bench, including Lord Wodehouse of Witton Hall, Lt-Col Petre of Westwick Hall and Edward Cubitt (Chairman) of Honing Hall. Clerk of the Court was Herbert William Thackeray Empson of Grammar School Road.

The Chief Constable, Capt Stephen Van Neck MC, sits proudly in the centre, with the town's Superintendent, Herbert Carter, at the Annual Inspection, *c.* 1933. Assembled for the group photograph are all the police officers for North Walsham and district; their beats and police houses covered most of North Norfolk, ranging from Aylsham to Neatishead and Itteringham to Potter Heigham.

North Walsham Cottage Hospital, *c.* 1938. Opened on 27 August 1924 by HRH Princess Marie Louise, the hospital was built on money provided by public subscription, amounting to over £9,000, as a permanent memorial to the 179 men of North Walsham and district who died during the First World War.

North Walsham's first motor ambulance, a converted horse-drawn Norwich Corporation wagon, in front of the Cottage Hospital ready to transport its very first patient to Bury St Edmunds, November 1927. It was driven by Ambulanceman William Oughton (left), accompanied by Divisional Superintendent 'G.B.' Fuller (closing the door).

Park House, on the corner of New Road and Pound Road, *c.* 1904. Towering up behind the house is the chimney (and to the left of the photograph the entrance gates) of W. & F. Press, the brewers, maltsters and hop merchants. After the death of Edward Press, the brewery site was sold along with the entire North Walsham & Dilham Canal. Held on Wednesday 11 September 1907, the sale comprised eight lots, including Wayford Bridge Granaries, Bacton Wood Mill and exclusive rights to pleasure boat traffic on the canal.

Washing cans at the Park Hall Works of Norfolk Canneries Ltd, 1937. Established in 1931 by Messrs Corbett & Duncan, Norfolk Canneries marketed locally produced fruit and vegetables tinned under the Duncan brand name. By 1938 the company's annual turnover exceeded £43,000, giving it the means to buy Park Hall and the new site at Millfield where, after a number of buy-outs, canned food is still produced today.

Children pause for the photographer on New Road, *c.* 1908. The road can be seen as straight and true, indicating its origins as an estate road. It was built by prisoners taken during the Napoleonic Wars and in the care of Capt Thomas Cooper. He set them the task of constructing roads around his estate known as The Oaks, which occupied most of the site now used as the town's War Memorial Park and the High School playing field.

Payne's Sweetshop, *c.* 1945. Built as a sweetshop and family home by Tom Payne in 1937, the business received a steady stream of customers from the nearby Regal Cinema, looking for a handy place to leave their bikes (behind the shop for the price of a penny) as well as for confectionery. The first company vehicle was a Jowett Bradford, shown here in front of the shop. The Bradford not only did the local rounds, but also delivered Ernie Hudson and his orchestra to local gigs. (Tom Payne's son, Dennis, played double bass in the orchestra.)

Church Street, *c.* 1937. These shops and businesses were run by some real local characters, among them William Griston, the tailor, at No. 8, dear old Arnold Pitcher, the newsagent and stationer, from whom many bought their first packet of Woodbines or Craven 'A', and Sid Sexton, who kept The White Swan (and who went on to keep the butcher's on Church Plain), its sign proudly boasting its Bullard's Ales. Just beyond the public house is the old premises of Bloom's Butchers, kept for generations by the Bloom family and renowned for its fine array of game strung along its window in the winter.

Carl Farrow, the Hall Lane blacksmith, 1938. Well over 100 years of smithing were shared by Carl and his father, William, at the forge on Hall Lane. Leaving school at thirteen, Carl went straight to his father's blacksmith shop to learn the trade. Always a keen horseman, Carl's proud claim was that he was the first man from North Walsham to join The King's Own Royal Regiment, Norfolk Imperial Yeomanry. When he left that service he served in the town's volunteer fire brigade for almost thirty years.

North Walsham Steam Laundry, *c.* 1902. The laundry was begun in 1900 with Mr and Mrs J.A. Ogilvy as managers. Surviving a fire in 1906, the business was rebuilt and grew to be known across North Norfolk as 'The High Class Family Laundry'. Its vans collected hotel laundry from places as far apart as Norwich and Mundesley.

The Shrubbery, 20 Cromer Road, 1929. This house was owned at the turn of the century by Walter Pallett, one of the partners in Barclay Pallett & Co., and was sold to the Fernie family after his death. It was sold again in the 1920s to Dr James Duncan Hart, who based his surgery there. His successors to both house and practice were Drs Thomas and Margaret McLeod. One of their close friends and frequent visitors was Agatha Christie, the renowned murder and mystery authoress who wrote at least two of her novels during her stays there. Today the magnificent building has been lovingly restored to most of its former glory and is now the popular local hotel The Beechwood.

This beautifully animated view of Cromer Road, complete with delivery boy and baskets and the bakery roundsman and his cart beyond, dates from about 1912. No. 8 Cromer Road was 'The Rising Sun', one of the country's smallest public houses, founded at the turn of the century by John Lancaster.

John B. Martin's fish merchant's, 4 Aylsham Road, *c.* 1927. Established during the mid-1920s, Martin's sold fresh North Sea fish as well as dried fish, which was smoked on the premises, while next door they opened a small fried fish shop, frying every night and all day Thursday. Known in later years as Ann's Fish Bar, it is now the Angel Bookshop.

The grand reopening of the Norwich Co-operative Society on Market Street in 1921. The original much smaller building, with pull-down blinds and an open drain running in front of it, was occupied by the Co-op from 1906 until it was burnt down while commandeered by the military during the First World War. Rebuilt after the end of the war, the Co-op grew into a well-established business and was sadly missed when it closed in 1983.

Photographed in the yard off Mundesley Road, behind the store, are roundsmen and staff of the Norwich Co-operative Society perched on the shop's bread delivery handcart, c. 1935. Left to right: Ben Curtis, George Wright (Mmanager), Mr Haggeth, -?-, Bob Hedge, Bob Lines, Mr Stretman, who was bread delivery roundsman.

Looking up Market Street, *c.* 1904. This evocative scene reflects the town when life went by at a slower pace and children could stand quite safely on roads where today traffic rushes by. Chimney pots, indicating the prevalent use of solid fuel, litter the skyline, especially in the centre of the picture where the houses in The Butchery stood. Running along both sides of the road are open sewers that worked on the declivity towards Mundesley Road, passed under Fayers' Bakery in the old barrel drain to the water course, and on to Catch Pit Lane.

Billy Howlett's fish shop and restaurant at 18 Market Street was begun by his father, George, in the 1890s. In 1949, when this photograph was taken, Billy wished to diversify. The shop was sold as a going business and was run for many years by the Jarvis brothers. Billy bought his house on Bacton Road with the money and began his coal delivery business, which grew and flourished. His distinctive dark green lorries, once familiar across the town, helped to develop his business yet further as he established a successful removals firm.

Bob Palmer's butcher's shop at 9 Market Street, *c.* 1900. Bob Palmer is standing in the doorway wearing the traditional butcher's stripy apron. He established his business here in the 1880s, passing the trade on to his son Charles, who took over the business in 1912. He ran the shop until just after the Second World War when it was bought by Don Kent.

Albert Edward Porter's jeweller's and watchmaker's at 12 Market Street, *c.* 1912. In the early 1920s the business moved to 45 Market Place and was subsequently sold to Len Hancock in the 1930s. Although it has changed hands a couple of times since then, the premises is still a jeweller's after over seventy years.

The view as it was down Market Street, *c.* 1930. On the right is the well-remembered Old Bear Stores, kept for many years by Albert Ernest Bloomfield. The store stocked all manner of groceries, provisions, wines and spirits. Some of the store's notoriety no doubt came from its early history as a centre where cock fighting, bare knuckle fighting and bear-baiting took place.

Market Street, viewed from the corner of the Market Place, *c.* 1950. In those days the sweet shop, run by Mr Chapman, was situated next door to the china and glass department of Blyth's, the long-established ironmongery store that stood round the corner. Woolcraft House sold childrenswear and housed Miss Mable Palmer's ladies' hairdressers. Beneath the signs for Hercules, Raleigh, Humber and Rudge cycles was Griffin's cycle shop, which was also one of the first stockists of televisions in the town. Far right is the fondly remembered Webb's fishing tackle and sporting goods shop with its well-stocked window display.

As Cubitt's store in the Market Place grew, his son and grandsons joined the firm forming Messrs Cubitt & Son Ltd. A number of these directors stand pictured in the doorway of their newly opened Grocery & Provision Stores on King's Arms Street, *c.* 1905. A further development came after the First World War when this branch specialized in the unusual combination of tinned food, furnishings and floor coverings.

North Walsham post office, King's Arms Street, *c.* 1908. Many local people recognize the distinctive frontage but I wonder how many have noticed the plaque above the window – a memorial to North Walsham Town Hall, which stood on the site for many years until 27 August 1899. On that morning smoke was seen coming from the building; the fire brigade was summoned but found its hose reels could not source any flow of water. Jockey Elvin, one of Robert Walpole Palmer's fastest riders from the King's Arms, was sent around the local farms to despatch water carts. Despite thirty carts bringing water from the canal within the hour, sadly the hall was lost. Rebuilt by John Dixon, the local auctioneer, it became first The Manor Hotel and eventually the post office and employment exchange.

.. THE ..

Picturedrome

King's Arms St., NORTH WALSHAM.

᛫᛫

North Walsham Picturedrome Co.
Manager - - *H. P. Coates*

Latest and Best Pictures.

Always a GOOD SHOW. ASK OUR PATRONS.

Monday to Friday nightly at 7.30.
Saturday night continuous from 6.30.

Admission 2/-, 1/6, 1/- and 6d.

Reduced Prices to all seats Wednesdays and Fridays. Best seats bookable – no extra charge. **ENTIRE CHANGE of PICTURES MONDAYS and THURSDAYS.**

Support your Theatre and get into the habit of at least one visit per week. The better the Theatre is patronised the Greater the Attractions.

A 1927 advert for 'The Picturedrome', North Walsham's first cinema, built in 1912 by Mr Nixon on King's Arms Street. The cinema, under the energetic management of Mr H.P. Coates, could seat 400, with features being shown Monday to Saturday. Saturday was always popular with local children, who could obtain entry with payment in eggs, rabbit pelts or jam jars. Sadly the old cinema was unable to compete with the new Regal when it opened on New Road in 1931 and it closed within a week.

Frederick Gregory's family grocer's, Excelsior House, King's Arms Street, 1904. Frederick established his business in the 1860s on Lower Street. After a short spell on Market Street he settled on King's Arms Street. Not only was he a popular grocer, but he also acted as registrar of births, deaths and marriages for the Smallburgh District, a job his son Ernest eventually took over. Having expanded his premises to stock beers and wines, Frederick sold the business to Arthur Cobbin in 1929, who was joined in partnership in the early '30s by Edward Newman and thus the well-remembered grocery store of Cobbin & Newman was established.

King's Arms Street, c. 1910. For many years this street was known as Norwich Road, bordered to the left with field land until the late eighteenth century when the road was improved and became the final leg of the Norwich to North Walsham Turnpike. Its final stop was The King's Arms Coaching Inn, kept in its heyday by Robert Walpole Palmer.

CHAPTER TWO

THE MARKET PLACE

The Market Cross, c. 1905, the undoubted centre-piece of North Walsham. It was built in the middle of the
sixteenth century by Bishop Thirlby to replace 'an earlier crumbling structure', possibly a monument to the
suppression of the Peasants' Revolt that saw its nemesis in the town centre in 1381.
Thirlby's cross was almost completely destroyed in the great fire of 1600 but was rebuilt by Bishop Redman
in 1602. Ownership of the cross passed to the Ecclesiastical Commissioners in 1830, who later sold it to the
town together with the market rights. It was restored in 1856 and extensively renovated in 1899, when the
clock and bell were installed by the Urban District Council at a total cost of £300.

Looking across the lower Market Place from The King's Arms, *c.* 1905. On the left, John Knights, the Southrepps market gardener and greengrocer, has drawn up his horse and cart to make a delivery to Arthur William 'Jammy' Loveless's grocer's. On the right, we can see William Alexander Le Grice's large general outfitter's, hatter's, boot and shoe store with its excellent window display.

Cubitt's Stores, Jubilee House, 21–2 Market Place, *c.* 1905. Established in 1835 by Charles Cubitt as a draper's and grocer, the business grew rapidly and spread to the adjoining premises. The building was refurbished and refaced at the time of Queen Victoria's Jubilee, and was renamed Jubilee House. This magnificent store included departments for ladies', gents' and children's outfitters, millinery, and funeral furnishings.

Frank Loads and William Loads jnr stand proudly in front of their newly refurbished draper's shop, *c.* 1907. This shop, once The Falcon public house, was originally purchased by their parents, William and Anne, for the grand sum of £485 when they moved from their smaller premises on Church Street in 1858.

Frank (standing, centre of the back row) and William Loads jnr (far left) with their workshop and shop staff, *c.* 1905. Upwards of thirty men were once employed in the workshops, either tailoring or boot making. Not only was high quality footwear produced, but also agricultural labourers' 'Highlows', astutely priced at 12*s.* – the exact weekly wage of such labourers. Many of the Loads' workforce were nicknamed by some locals as 'dummies' as they were deaf mutes. They worked an unusual week, from Tuesday to Saturday, because they got so drunk on Sunday evening they were unfit for work on a Monday morning!

Mr Robinson and Jack Fiddy standing in the office doorway of Herbert Plumbley FAI auctioneer, estate agent, valuer and cattle salesman, 30 Market Place, 1932. His main sale ground was the cattle market on Yarmouth Road, although his office officiated at sales all around the district as indicated by posters in his window, which advertise forthcoming sales at Southrepps, Felmingham, Banningham Hall and Swafield.

Fuller's draper's, Norfolk House, 1925. A draper's for over 200 years, this was a shop of many firsts. It was the first shop in North Walsham to have gas installed and one of the first to have a telephone; it was here that the first meetings of the North Walsham Division of St John Ambulance Brigade were held in the back room under the auspices of George Burton 'GB' Fuller, the shop's owner and town's first St John Superintendent. In those days people who rang up received the unusual greeting of 'Drapery or Ambulance?'

Sewell & Page's butcher's shop, 35 Market Place, *c.* 1910. The business was founded by Thomas Sewell, butcher and corn dealer, in the 1880s at 29 Market Place. Joined in partnership by Walter Page just after the turn of the century, they moved shortly after to the larger premises pictured here. In the 1920s it became W. Page & Co. Family Butchers, carrying on the fine tradition of supplying beef, mutton, lamb, game, home-cured hams and bacon to the local populace until the 1940s.

What am I bid? A crowd, including the local police officer, gathers around the old town pump in the Market Place to hear the street auctioneer, *c.* 1903.

Dan Mount sluicing the drains by water barrow in the Market Place, *c.* 1910. Before the days of flush toilets and piped disposal of sewerage the town was beset with the problems of smelly street gutters, especially in the Market Place and down on to Market Street and particularly on hot days. Dan, often assisted by 'Bruff' Hewitt, was employed by the Urban District Council to 'flush and brush' the gutters down daily. William Morris, the town surveyor, reported in 1932 that the 'noxious and offensive effluvia from such filth' was soaking into the rotting joints between the bricks; as an elementary step large quantities of sanitary fluid was used so the ' . . . stench of sewage gave off a pretty reassuring smell of disinfectant'. The long awaited stormwater drainage and sewerage disposal scheme was laid down in 1927. For those not on the scheme the system of night soil collection was 'greatly improved' with the purchase of a new rubber-tyred 'honey' cart!

The busy Market Place, *c.* 1933. The general shape of the place has not really changed but the businesses once familiar to all residents certainly have. In those days, Peacock's Penny Bazaar was at the top of the town on Church Plain; to the right were The Cross Keys Inn, Randell's ironmonger's, George Gaze's baker's & confectioner's, Curry's cycles, James Smith's dryer's & cleaner's, London Central Meat Company, Thomas Burton's ironmonger's and the only one still there today – Barclays Bank.

Barker's draper's shop in Waterloo House dominates the lower Market Place, *c.* 1932. Built at the turn of the nineteenth century, the house was christened after Wellington's final defeat of Napoleon at Waterloo in 1815. Run for most of its life as a temperance hotel, it was purchased in the 1900s by Benjamin Barker for his draper's, milliner's and outfitter's store. The business was run by him until just after the Second World War, when it was sold to Edward Reid who ran it as The Loke House. In more recent years it was R. Edmonds & Son Ltd Hardware Store. It is now the Waterloo Stores produce centre.

Marjoram Brothers' gentlemen's outfitters, 42 Market Place, *c.* 1903. Mr Fred Marjoram founded the business in 1901 and was joined by his brother Frank in 1912. As partners they opened an additional premises on Church Street as a drapery (now Paperchain). After many years running the two businesses they closed the drapery and sold the building. During the war Frank died but Fred carried on the business, ably assisted by his married daughter, Mrs Doris Rayner. Her husband Herbert joined as business partner in 1946, and on Fred's death he took over the business. In 1962 Mr Lawrence Polley joined the business and he soon became a partner; in 1977 he bought out Mr Rayner's share. Sadly the shop closed in 1988 after eighty-seven years of continuous trading.

Randell's ironmonger's shop, 5 Market Place, *c.* 1910. Established in the early nineteenth century, the shop passed from generation to generation to become one of the oldest established family shops in the town. The frontage with its wonderful display of hardware and lamps dates from the late 1890s when Randell's became a limited firm and the old bow-fronted shop was modernized and refitted. Sadly the shop closed in the 1980s and is now The Drugstore.

The ruined tower of the Parish Church of St Nicholas, *c.* 1910. The tower once stood at the magnificent height of 147 ft, and was topped with a lead spire (erected after the completion of the 160 ft Cromer Church tower – townspeople would not be outdone!). On Friday 15 May 1724 the town held its Ascension Day Fair and the bells were rung all day. The tower was greatly weakened and it swiftly collapsed the following morning. Somewhat more of the tower was left than we see today until the extreme gales of February 1836, when most of the extant north side of the steeple was blown down. Luckily there have been no further dramatic falls to date. Things have changed since this photo was taken; the iron railings around the grave yard were salvaged for the war effort and the tombstones were moved to the side walls a few years later.

Local auctioneer Capt John Dixon FALPA, appointed in 1882 as organist to St Nicholas' Parish Church, pictured *c.* 1932. When he was first given the position he played on the old organ erected in about 1873 by Hill & Son of London. He is pictured with the new organ, which had 3 manuals, 44 stops and 14 accessories. It was erected in a different position (the old organ space is now occupied by the War Memorial Chapel) in 1913 at a cost of £965 by Norman & Beard of Norwich.

Some of the volunteer 'Mrs Mopps' giving the ancient choir stalls inside St Nicholas' Church an extra special clean and polish in preparation for its rededication service in September 1966.

CHAPTER THREE

LOST NORTH WALSHAM

Much of the old town of North Walsham has not simply changed but, tragically, has been lost forever. The Oaks was one of the first major 'casualties' of modern times, in the 1930s. Built in the eighteenth century by Thomas Cooper on the site of an earlier great house owned by the Withers family, The Oaks remained with the Cooper family until it was purchased by Revd Tilney Spurdens upon his retirement from the Grammar School. After passing through a number of hands it became dilapidated and the site is now occupied by the post office and community centre.

Eric Harmer, the affectionately remembered local reporter, is joined by two young lads as he watches the tearing down of Hospital Yard opposite the Salvation Army Citadel on Hall Lane. The worst destruction of the old town came in the late 1950s and 1960s when most of the buildings and yards in and around Hall Lane and Vicarage Street were flattened.

The view across the demolished area that was Dog Yard (so named after The Dog public house, which had stood there during the nineteenth century), showing the houses at the junction of Vicarage Street and lower Bacton Road, c. 1959. The site was converted into Reeves Court, residential flats for local elderly folk.

Wright's stores on the corner of Vicarage Street and Back Street, *c.* 1958. This whole block and area were demolished to make way for the Vicarage Street car park.

The view up Bacton Road from the corner of Back Street, *c.* 1958. On the left, at No. 1, was Charlie Grey's hardware store, furniture dealer's and tobacconist's begun by his father in the 1920s. The shop became typical of those in the area, diversifying to stock all manner of household items from candles to clothes pegs.

Looking up the leafy and quiet Back Street, *c.* 1958. Again this has all been demolished to make way for the car park. We are very lucky to have this pictorial record of the lost streets, captured by several local people when news broke that the area was going to be demolished. Probably the most comprehensive photographic study was undertaken by the late Mr Jack Hewitt, many of whose pictures appear herein.

Stephen Hewitt stands proudly in the doorway of his newly opened butcher's shop that stood on the junction of North Street and Mundesley Road in 1932. A popular local butcher, he ran his shop for thirty years without a day's sickness or holiday. Shortly after his retirement in 1962 the shop was demolished to enable the road to be widened.

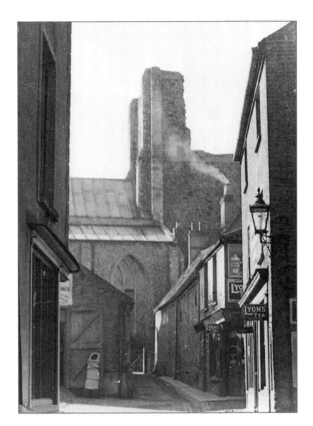

The top of North Street looking towards Church Plain, *c.* 1904. The early emergency services of the town were based here with the old fire-house, which stored the 1743 Newsham Pump engine, on Cock Street and the original police station and lock-up, built in 1846, on Theatre Street. During the twentieth century the old ambulance house was on Church Plain.

On the corner of North Street, at 33 Vicarage Street, was one of the most affectionately remembered shops in the history of North Walsham. Kept by a real Norfolk character – Eva May Kimm (right), pictured with her dear friend Mrs MacLean, *c.* 1930 – this shop stocked everything from soles for shoes to sacks of potatoes, kindling, sweets and Corona lemonade.

Vicarage Street from Church Plain, *c.* 1950. Well-scrubbed doorsteps and neat terraced houses epitomize the community that inhabited this old area of the town. The street itself has been known as Church Gate, Church Street, Theatre Street and finally Vicarage Street. The name of Theatre Street was derived from David Fisher's theatre, which was built as part of his theatre 'circuit' at the beginning of the nineteenth century. The building later became the town's first National School (1846), divided by a great curtain with boys on one side and girls on the other. Later still, as the Church Rooms, it was the venue for many fine local festivities and amateur theatrical performance. Today it is a kitchen showroom.

Beside Frank Chittock's footwear shop, running beside Vicarage Street, was the loke to Ship Yard (named after the ancient pub which once backed on to it), pictured *c.* 1955. The yard was filled with old weavers' cottages complete with wide windows to make the most of the hours of daylight. This has all been demolished to make way for the shopping precinct.

The Congregational Church Sunday school hall, *c.* 1895. It was converted from the old Congregational Chapel after their move to the new and bigger gothic building on Cromer Road. This building met its fate in the 1960s to make way for the shopping precinct.

Mitre Tavern Yard, known in the eighteenth century as Maid's Head Yard after the old pubs it once backed on to, is pictured in about 1955. This yard was well known to local children, who would delight in watching the town's last blacksmith, Ernie Turner, at work in his forge here.

General view of Randell's Foundry on Bacton Road, c. 1950. Opened as the St Nicholas Works by Frank and Horace Randell in 1865, it became known as F. Randell Ltd when Horace left in the 1890s. Under Frank 'The Guv'nor's' guidance and innovative flair for machinery design the business flourished as one of the premier agricultural machinery manufacturers in Norfolk well into the twentieth century.

A comparative view of Randell's Foundry being torn down in 1988. Time has marched on. Randell's was subject to a number of take-overs and eventually moved to North Walsham Industrial Estate while the old foundry site was sold for development. The latter is now a Somerfields supermarket. When I went to record this sad occasion, walking through the deserted workshops my ears rang with the silence enforced on the hard-worked benches; a history of 100 years of agricultural machinery making and iron founding was in those walls, now knocked down and gone forever.

CHAPTER FOUR

SCHOOL DAYS

Paston Grammar School, c. 1930, the oldest extant school in the town. Built on land laid waste by the great fire of 1600, the school was founded as a Free School by the benevolent Sir William Paston in 1606. Its popularity and success necessitated its enlargement and new schoolhouses replaced the old in 1765 and 1828. Further extensions came in 1928 (the new schoolrooms pictured here on the right) and in 1939.

The masters and boys of Tenison House, Paston Grammar School, *c.* 1914. The house system was set up in 1911 by the then headmaster George Hare to encourage competition. Each house took its name from a notable 'Old Pastonians', these being Bishop Tenison, Wharton, Nelson and Hoste. In those days tuition fees were £8 per annum; boarders paid £33 per annum, exclusive of books and tuition, with an admission fee of £1 1*s.* Day boys who lived at a distance could dine in the schoolhouse four days a week at £2 10*s.* per term.

Paston Grammar School Cadet Corps Guard of Honour being inspected by Lord Eustace Percy, President of the Board of Education, when he came to open the new school block on 3 October 1928. He is accompanied by Capt F.H. Brown MC and Maj Percival Pickford DSO, MC, TD, MA (headmaster).

Paston Grammar School 1st XI Football Team, 1951/2 season. Back row, left to right: D.G. Woodhouse, Amis, W.C. Craske, Griston, R.R. Sadler, J.R. Duffield. Front row: B. Hodgson, M.S. Home, N.R. Keeler (captain), N.G. Haig, Tillet. A very successful team: in that season they played 19 games, won 13, drew 2 and lost 4.

Paston Grammar School Under 14 Cricket XI, 1952, in front of the pavilion on the school field. Back row, left to right: V. Hunter (scorer), Berry, Crowe, Hammond, Craske, Gilliland, Randell, R. Hunter (umpire). Front row; Carver, Nelson, Abel, Henson, Daniels.

Paston Grammar School first ever 1st Hockey XI, 1952/3. Back row, left to right: Lingwood, Troller, Goldson, Belson, Bartram, Gant. Front row: Howard, Walker, Dixon, Paterson, MacLean.

Paston Grammar School Senior Athletic Team, 1953. Back row, left to right: R. Craske, B.J. Brooke, E. Rump, *c.* Bunn, A.R. Paterson. Front row: N. Gant, G.V. Griston, D.G. Amis, R. Harrison, R. Fenn.

The Girls' High School, The Lawn, *c.* 1921. The school had been run as a private girls' school since 1903 by Misses Jane and Maria Cook. It was taken over by Norfolk Education Committee in 1919 and the following year was recorded as having 70 pupils and 3 mistresses.

A fine portrait of young ladies from the Girls' High School, *c.* 1928. They are all wearing their shields, the first letters denoting which house they belonged to. Each house was named after one of the four Marys who were ladies-in-waiting to Mary, Queen of Scots. Each house also had its own motto – thus: Beaton, 'Through Combat to Victory'; Carmichael, 'Play up and Play the Game'; Hamilton, 'Excelsior'; and Seaton, 'Perseverando'.

It all looks very St Trinian's! No doubt these girls were much more well behaved at their Prize Day in 1952. One old girl (1951–8) – Mrs Gillian Shephard MP (née Watts) – recalls that the summer dresses all the girls are seen wearing ' . . . were strictly controlled. There was one legendary girl who was reputed to have a dozen green and white dresses, each deviating just a little from the regulation and declared unfit by vigilant staff.'

Miss M.S. Middlewood BA, headmistress of the Girls' High School from 1947 to 1967, gives the address at Prize Day, 1953. During her incumbency the number of pupils increased from about 250 to about 400, and the sixth form from 16 to 65.

The Girls' High School Senior Choir and Orchestra in the old gym, 1954. The choirs were supervised and directed by the tireless Miss Gosling. There were junior and senior choirs as well as a morning choir, which led the singing in assemblies, and a madrigal choir, which eventually made a record.

A costume drama at the Girls' High School, c. 1953. Dramatic productions and revues were frequently staged and were popular with students and parents. A number were written and produced by the multi-talented Miss Ali. If the weather permitted, it was desirable for these events to be held in the open air as the old gym could not comfortably accommodate the performers as well as the audience.

The garden at the rear of Beech Grove House, with the school sanitorium in the background on New Road, *c.* 1915. During the war the school gardener was called up, and boarders were allocated a plot to 'dig for victory' and produce vegetables.

The Council School, Manor Road, *c.* 1905. (To the right may be seen the wall of the old town pound where stray farm animals were 'gated' until collection; now demolished, it is remembered in the name of Pound Road.) The school, built by Mr R. Cornish for £3,300, was funded by the School Board and opened in 1874 to accommodate 500 children.

North Walsham Junior School, Class 2, *c.* 1919. The school was greatly enlarged between 1888 and 1903 at a total cost of £5,400 to hold 274 junior boys, 210 junior girls and 200 infants. In 1909 the new mixed junior school (pictured) was opened, complete with woodwork and housecraft rooms.

Boys' Department Choir, *c.* 1920. Under the three masters – Mr William Kemp, instructor of the Boys' Orchestra, assisted by Mr Clifford 'Snag' Anstiss, all under the direction of Mr A.W. Colthorpe, the headmaster – the choir won two first prizes in the Norwich and Norfolk Musical Festival.

North Walsham Council School Football Team, 1929. Back row, left to right: Clifford Anstiss (teacher), Les Reynolds, Stan Lowe, Billie Dawson, 'Whiffy' Catlin, Jack 'Smiler' Buck (caretaker). Middle row: Ernie Hedge, Archie Wright, Sid 'Tom' Thirtle, Joe Reynolds, Les Miles. Front row: Albert Lee and Reggie Miller.

One of the Central School's first sports days in the late 1930s. The headmaster, Mr Reginald Cubitt, trilby in hand, prepares to open proceedings. In those days local children who did not receive scholarships or have parents willing or able to pay for grammar school education went to school, from infants to seniors, on the one Manor Road site. Opened in October 1938, the school's formal title was the Central Board Co-Educational School, which dispensed with the traditionally separate departments for boys and girls.

Pupils of the Secondary Modern School are assembled in the hall on the school's original site on Manor Road for Prize Day, *c.* 1952.

The Youth Centre was always a popular out of school activity. Seen here are some of its members while on their rounds bringing Christmas cheer to local people during the festive season, 1953.

Secondary Modern School Girls' Hockey Team, 1948/9 season.

Secondary Modern School Junior Netball Team, 1958/9. Back row, left to right: Sandra Howard, Jill Powell, Gillian Bane, Dorothy Cousins. Front row: Diane Storey, Rosilind Camoron, Pauline Drury, Sarah Drury, Gillian Hicks.

On your marks! The young ladies are ready for the sprint at the Secondary Modern School sports day, 1951.

Mr George Howard (PE master), far left, stands proudly with the Secondary Modern School Junior Football XI, 1958/9 season.

The boys are off to a good start on the Secondary Modern School cross-country race, *c.* 1962. Always setting off with good intentions, it would not be long before the mud splashed up their legs and caked their boots like lead. Most of the old school cross-country route has now been used for housing development – town schoolchildren today just don't know how lucky they are!

Tackling the water obstacle. 'Chip' Bowerin marshalls the boys across during the 1962 school cross-country race.

CHAPTER FIVE

CLUBS & SOCIETIES

North Walsham Draughts Club, 1893. Back row, left to right: C. Simpson, W. Claxton, J. Adams, W. Green, S. Jarvis, R. Pigott, A. Barnes, W. Worts, J. Worts, W. Hart, F. Breese. Front row: M. Dodman, J. Blyth, J. Starling, Vice-President F. Davies, President Dr Shepherd, J. Waters, W. Rance (seated, cross-legged), W. Dyball, Z. Priest, N. Church (seated on ground, legs outstretched), R. Knights.

North Walsham Salvation Army Youth Band, 1936. The town has had close associations with the Salvation Army since the unit was opened here on 1 August 1885 under the command of Capt Fanny Evans.

In addition to the band, which still flourishes today, North Walsham Salvation Army had a very fine company of songsters, pictured here in about 1960. How many do you recognize?

'Round the camp-fire' at their HQ in the Youth Centre on Park Lane are the 1st North Walsham Scouts in 1952. Their leaders are standing along the back wall; on the far right are the Scoutmasters Mr Alec 'Dickie' Bird and Mr Cyril Griffin (the author's great-uncle).

North Walsham Girl Guides, *c.* 1925.

North Walsham Girls' Friendly Society Dancing Team, ready for their trip to dance for the Queen Mother at the Royal Albert Hall, June 1950. Left to right: Nancy Spinks, Jean Manning, Phyl Scott, Christine Foulser, Joyce Wright, Josie Cutting, Phyl Wright, Sadie Bartrum (ready to courtsey), Janet Pitt, Pamela Fayers, Faphne Neave, Edna Scott, Phyllis Harris, Beth Cubitt, Cynthia Matthews and Kay Bowman. It is good to note that 'Edna's Dancing Girls' still have reunions to date.

Members of the town's newly founded (April 1924) St John Ambulance Brigade and reorganized (1926) Women's Voluntary Aid Detachment, British Red Cross Society, after the Annual Inspection, 1928. Back row, left to right: Ptes Dack, Dixon, Gee, Dunton, Bird, Claydon, Watts, Allard. Front row: Pte Oughton, Nurses Cooper and Ferrier, Divisional Superintendent 'G.B.' Fuller, Assistant Commissioner Barclay, Commissioner Maj Hossack, County Superintendant Emms, Sgt Cooper and Nurse Coles.

North Walsham St John Ambulance Brigade members and cadets after church parade, *c.* 1968.

A young cadet sergeant from 2110 (North Walsham) Squadron Air Training Corps is presented with his proficiency certificate in the Market Place, *c.* 1952.

'This little piggy went . . .' not to market but to the Young Farmers' pet show, held on the school playing field, October 1950.

Sunday school young people's tea held in the Methodist Church Hall on Grammar School Road, 1950.

One of many award presentations at North Walsham Youth Club, 1954. Run under the guidance of the Norfolk Education Committee by Mr and Mrs G.B. Howard, the club was based on Park Lane and open from 7 to 10 p.m. on Mondays, Tuesdays and Thursdays with an extra long evening during the summer months.

When the Youth Club first acquired its premises on Park Lane its members carried out much of the restoration work themselves. In the same tradition, any further decoration or work was done by the members, as seen here when the interior was refreshed by a coat of paint in 1956.

North Walsham Town Football Club after a match on their station field pitch, *c.* 1925.

North Walsham 'Hornets' Football Club, 1928/9 season. Back row, left to right: A. Hick, L. Roper, L. Nutman, D. Youngman, W. Cork, J. Woods, V. Willey, W. Branch. Middle row: P. Steward, S. Riches, L. White, *c.* Watts, G. Bush, A. Andrews, W. Chamberlain, B. Starling. Front row: W. Rayner, C. Whitwood, E. Plummer, E. Allen.

North Walsham ladies' cricket team, *c.* 1952. Back row, left to right: Joyce Wright, Mary Wade, Jane Morgan, Valerie Bush, Hazel Page, Sylvia Yaxley. Front row: Edith Cutting, Elizabeth Page, Kay Bowman, Phyl Scott, Joy Mokes, Nancy Spinks. One of the team's most light-hearted matches was when they played the town's male XI. To make it a bit more even, the men had only two wickets to aim at and when they came to bat they had to use the opposite hand to which they were accustomed. Sadly the ladies still lost by 20 runs.

Members of North Walsham and District Athletic Association, *c.* 1959. Affiliated to the Amateur Athletic Association and Norfolk County AAA, the club organized an annual sports meeting. One of many Norfolk championships, this meeting was built up to be one of the leading events in the county and attracted contenders from all over the country.

Members of North Walsham old folks' club are ready and waiting in the Market Place for the coach to collect them as they leave for their annual beano to Great Yarmouth in July 1949.

North Walsham Private Bowling Club, winners of 1st Division Norfolk County Cup, 1933. Back row, left to right: W.F. Loynes, W.T. Pearce, E.E. Symonds, G.G. Bloom, A.W. Colthorpe, W. Storey, H.T. Youell, F. Marjoram. Front row: L. Dunton, W.G. Robinson, F.J. Miles, G. Smart (President), W. Mace, S. Watts, A. Cutting, G. Howlett.

CHAPTER SIX

EVENTS & OCCASIONS

The Church Rooms on Vicarage Street, packed with locals enjoying the 'Any Questions' evening that was just one of a number of special entertainments laid on for North Walsham Shopping Week, 1952.

North-Walsham,
SECOND FESTIVAL.
IN COMMEMORATION OF
PEACE,
THE 19th. JULY, 1814.

In the Afternoon immediately after Dinner, there will be
the following Sports and Amusements,

A Donkey Race,

For a Pannel Saddle, Value One Pound to be given to the first winner of two Heats.
A Bridle with a blue Ribband, value 12 Shillings to the second winner of two Heats.
No fewer then Six or more than Eight Donkies, will be permitted to run

The Donkies may come from any part of the Universe, and must be entered at the
King's Arms Inn, before Nine o'clock on Tuesday Morning.

A Jumping Match, by 12 Men,

Each Man to Jump in a Four Bushel Sack One Hundred Yards.
The best jumper to have a Hat, value One Pound The second best a Hat, value 8 shillings.
The Men to Provide their own Sacks, and to enter their Names at the King's Arms
Inn before Nine o'clock on Tuesday Morning

A Jingling Match.

For a Pair of Breeches value One Pound, and a pair of Stockings value 4 shillings
A Jingler with a Bell, to be placed in the centre of a roped square. Ten Men blindfold-
ed to be placed at equal distances between the Rope and the Bell ringer twenty Mi-
nutes to be allowed for the match. The Man who catches the Bell Ringer, to have the
Breeches, and the Bell-Ringer the stockings But if the Bell Ringer eludes all the Jinglers, both the prizes to be awarded to him

The best Runner for One Hundred Yards, to be the Bell Ringer.
The Jinglers to enter their Names at the King's Arms Inn, before Nine o'clock on
Tuesday Morning.

A CHEMISE RACE,

For a beautiful Chemise fashionably made, & handsomely decorated Value 20 shillings
A new Petticoat, tastefully made, & elegantly trimmed, Value 15 shillings.
A new and fascinating Blucher Cap, Value 8 shillings.
To be run for by Six Ladies - the distance 150 Yards and back - the best winner to
have the Chemise - the second best the Petticoat, and the third best the Cap.
Each of the blooming Racers will have her Hair Handsomely bound, & decorated with
two yards of Vittoria Ribband previously to starting.
The fair competitors to run in white Stockings, red petticoats, and white Jackets,
which will be provided for them by the committee of rustic sports.
The ladies to Enter their Names at Mr. WM. YOURD'S or Mr. WM. POWELL'S
before 9 o'clock on Tuesday Morning.

PLUMBLY, PRINTER N WALSHAM

Poster for the Second Festival in Commemoration of Peace with France, held in the town on 19 July
1814. A dinner consisting of roast beef, plum puddings, bread and ale was followed by the delights of the
rural sports listed above.

Public dinner in the Market Place in celebration of the Golden Jubilee of Queen Victoria, Tuesday 21 June 1887. Thirty-six 50 ft long tables were set up, each accommodating sixty people. Every table had a steward, 3 carvers, 4 to 6 waitresses and 2 beer carriers. The meal consisted of cold beef, two-thirds roast ribs and rump and one-third boiled and brisket, washed down with a pint of beer for men, half for women and ginger beer for 'Blue Ribboners' and children.

Children from the Board School singing in the Market Place to honour Queen Victoria's Golden Jubilee, Tuesday 25 June, 1897. Marched into position, the children sang 'God Save the Queen' and gave three cheers. Marched to the recreation ground, they received coronation commemorative medals, tickets for refreshments and a toy.

Another well-attended occasion was the annual parade of The Loyal Trafalgar Lodge of The Independent Order of Odd Fellows, Manchester Unity Friendly Society, pictured in September 1907. Dating back to the days when the Combination Acts forbade the forming of trade unions, these friendly societies provided benefits in time of sickness, disability or old age. At one time the town's branch counted over 500 members, with capital of over £30,000 in the 1950s.

The Coronation bullock, presented by Sewell and Pages' butchers, being exhibited in the Market Place on 15 June 1911 as part of the celebrations for the coronation of George V. Locals paid 2d. a go to guess its weight. The winner was George Mace; the weight was 71 stone 9 lb. George won a silver cup, presented by Frank Miles, the watchmaker.

The launch of the town's coronation celebrations at the Board School on Manor Road on 22 June 1911. Children were marshalled into their places by 9.40 a.m. and speeches were given by Revd Aubrey Aitken, Revd Mowbray Finnis and Mr Albert Walker. The chief event was the hoisting of the flag by Mrs Dixon to start the day. Two little girls, Peggy Snell and Hilda Ford, then presented Mrs Dixon with a bouquet of flowers. After the service the children filed into the school to receive their coronation mugs.

The town centre filled with tables and stewards again for the coronation celebrations of King George V and Queen Mary, 22 June 1911. In the centre of the crowd is the town band, who played to accompany singing of the Grace. John Dixon, the chairman of the festivities, invited those standing by, many of whom were wayfarers, to join and they were heartily welcomed. One old soldier who was on the tramp recalled with tears in his eyes that he had celebrated Queen Victoria's Golden Jubilee (in 1887) in India.

The assembled dignitaries in front of the old Paston Grammar School on 3 October 1928 for the opening of the new additional school building, which had been built at a total cost of £8,700. Left to right: Frederick Bell (Clerk to the School Governors), Revd H.H. Thorns, R.W. Ketton-Cremer, Sir Reginald Neville of Sloley Hall, Revd R.J. Tacon, Mr D. Davidson (Chairman of the Norfolk Education Committee), The Dowager Lady Suffield, E.H. Evans-Lombe, -?-, Mr F.H. Barclay (Chairman of the Governors), Sydney Hare, Lord Eustace Percy (President of the Board of Education, who performed the opening ceremony), -?-, H.W.T. Empson, John Dixon JP, W.P. Case, Canon Aitken, -?- Albert Walker, -?-, -?-, -?-.

Sir Thomas Cook MP, President of the Norfolk Fire Brigade's Association, inspects the magnificent turnout of the various brigades from across Norfolk assembled in the Market Place as the town hosts their annual parade in 1937. He is accompanied by the town mayor and Capt W.J. Beck of Sennowe Park Brigade, who was parade marshal.

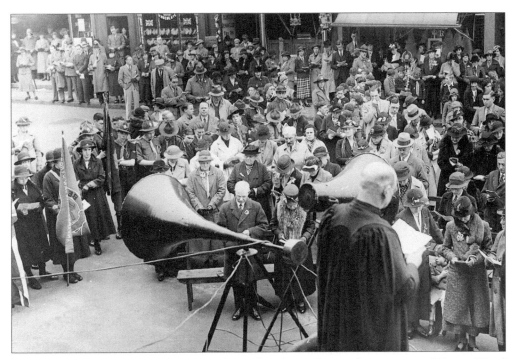

United service of prayer and thanksgiving in the Market Place to honour the coronation of George VI and Queen Elizabeth, 12 May 1937. Service papers were provided, and the singing accompanied by the Salvation Army Band. The loudspeakers were set up so that the crowds could listen to the coronation service, broadcast live from Westminster at 10.45 a.m. ' . . . for the benefit of those who do not have receiving sets'.

The coronation celebrations of 12 May 1937 continued all day with activities including a Grand Treasure Hunt, children's sports and an 'American Progressive Tennis Tournament'. There were no public tennis courts at the time, so Messrs Griston, Hare, Pallett and Walker lent their private courts. The festivities culminated in the Grand Evening Carnival; one of the floats is pictured here as it passes through the Market Place on its procession to the People's Park where a top prize of 20s. was to be awarded to the best decorated lorry or trade van.

Members of North Walsham St John Ambulance Brigade and British Red Cross Society on parade for the dedication of their new ambulance in the Market Place on Sunday 22 August 1948. Recording the event for posterity, perched on the ledge of his shop, is Roland Ling, the respected local chemist and photographer. His son Michael is watching from the window on the far right.

Revd R.H. Bradshaw gives the address at the launch of 'Battle of Britain Week', September 1953. The parade, which had marched through the town, was led by an RAF band with squads of RAF and WRAF personnel behind Sqdn Ldr T.S. Wilkinson. The second part of the parade was led by the Aylsham & District Silver Band followed by RAFA members from all over the district, who were in turn followed by numerous groups representing all the local uniformed organizations.

All eyes on the Market Cross at the opening of North Walsham Shopping Week, October 1952. An attraction was the investiture of the very first Miss North Walsham, Kay Bowman. Elected by popular ballot, she attended the functions and presented the prizes for entertainments and competitions during the week.

An outing of the North Walsham butchers ready to leave from the Market Cross, c. 1952. Back row (by the clock), left to right: Claude Leatherdale, Don Kent, Stephen Hewitt, Billy Baker. Middle row: Dick Smith, -?-, Walter Palmer, -?-, Fred Wright, Arthur Bloom, Freddy Bloom. Front row: Charlie Dadd with Kim the dog, Wilfred Lancaster, Allen Wright and Jack Gorrod.

A magnificent wedding breakfast spread at The Oaks' ballroom in Queen Elizabeth II's coronation year, 1952. Once a popular function room, The Oaks hosted all manner of dinner dances and 'socials' for local businesses, clubs and societies. Also well remembered are The Oaks' delicious pure ices, made by Mr Boldra, which the children enjoyed while their parents had morning coffee or afternoon tea.

Lieutenant-General Sir Terence Airey KCMG, CB, CBE receives the salute as members of the Royal British Legion parade through the Market Place led by their standards when the town hosted their county rally in 1976.

CHAPTER SEVEN

WAR

Men of L Company (North Walsham and District Detachment) 3rd Volunteer Battalion, The Norfolk Regiment on parade under command of Frederick Bunting, their Musketry Sergeant, in the Market Place on their return from serving in the Boer War, c. 1902. They are wearing khaki uniforms, Slade-Wallace webbing and distinctive slouch hats.

The First World War broke out on Tuesday 4 August 1914; all Regular Army troops were sent to their immediate war stations and the territorials were mobilized for war the same week. Local men were all touched by the pervading feeling of patriotic fervour. Many wanted to 'do their bit', answering the call of Kitchener's omnipresent finger under the banner of 'Britain Needs You!' He knew the war would not be over by Christmas and appealed for 100,000 men. Here the young men from North Walsham answer that call and march down Norwich Road, led by the town band and Recruiting Officer, to depart from the railway station to become 'Kitchener Volunteers'.

The 6th (Territorial Cyclist) Battalion, The Norfolk Regiment, HQ Company Signal Section, complete with semaphore flags, on their training area on The Oaks Estate near New Road, 1914.

Don't be Alarmed,
the Norfolks are on guard
at North Walsham.

The 6th (Territorial Cyclist) Battalion, The Norfolk Regiment was the first military unit to be stationed in the town during the First World War. The men arrived on 5 August 1914 and were billeted in the Board School. The town was to be their HQ. The Battalion, under the overall command of Col Bernard Henry Leathes Prior, was responsible for coastal defence duties and mounted patrols between Wells-on-Sea and Gorleston.

Norfolk Constabulary.

PUBLIC NOTICE.

DAYLIGHT
HOSTILE AIR RAIDS

When hostile aircraft are within such a distance of

NORTH WALSHAM

as to render an attack possible, the public will be warned thereof by the following signals:—

Each Day of the week (including Sunday)
"Danger" Signal.

Police and Special Constables will patrol the streets on cycles exhibiting cards bearing the words, "POLICE NOTICE, TAKE COVER."

The Constables will blow whistles frequently to attract attention.

"All Clear" Signal.

Police and Special Constables will patrol the streets on cycles exhibiting cards bearing the words, "POLICE NOTICE, ALL CLEAR."

The Constables will blow whistles frequently to attract attention.

The signals will be given during the period of **half-an-hour before sunrise to half-an-hour after sunset.** Every effort will be made to give **timely** warning of the approach of hostile aircraft, but the public should remember that the "**Danger**" signal will be given when **Real Danger** is apprehended in which event they should **Seek Shelter** with all speed.

Persons still in the open should take what shelter is afforded by lying in ditches, hollows in the ground, &c.

It is recommended that, in the event of raids during school hours, children should be kept in the school until the "**All Clear**" signal is given. Likewise, workpeople at factories, etc., should remain on the premises in whatever shelter is afforded.

Horses and other animals should be stabled or secured in some manner and should not be abandoned in the streets.

J. H. MANDER, Captain,
Chief Constable.

County Police Station,
Castle Meadow, Norwich,
January, 1918.

Poster warning of daylight air raids from Zeppelins, January 1918. The first aerial bombardment of civilian targets was carried out on the east coast towns of Sheringham, Great Yarmouth and King's Lynn on 19 January 1915. Further raids were carried out on Norfolk later in the war, the most notable on East Dereham on 9 September 1915. The county towns were constantly on their guard against further attacks until the end of the war.

Royal Naval Anti-Aircraft Mobile Brigade, complete with Rolls-Royce armoured cars and Royal Enfield motor cycles, on Yarmouth Road, April 1916. This detachment was based on Grammar School Road under Lt Mackenzie Ashton. Its job was to defend the coast from the Zeppelin menace, although following a number of coastal raids the German airships made London their target. Many an argument ensued between the mobile brigade and the captain of the Happisburgh light ship as they requested him to turn off the beacon because the Zeppelin pilots were using it as a guide.

The YMCA Soldiers' 'Hut', established in the Church Rooms on Vicarage Street, *c.* 1915. Open free of charge to all members of HM Forces, such huts were always popular meeting places for servicemen and were found all over the country and indeed in many overseas theatres of war. In North Walsham local boys remember waiting outside the hall to see if they could 'cadge a badge' from a soldier.

Nurses and convalescing soldiers at the Lower House Voluntary Aid Detachment Hospital, Mundesley Road, *c.* 1915. The house was handed over to become an auxiliary war hospital for convalescing servicemen for the duration of the war. Opening on 11 November 1914, the hospital provided just 11 beds and during the war admitted 714 patients. It had the distinction of being the last of many such auxiliary hospitals in the county to close, on 20 March 1919.

Edith Wilkinson Carter ARRC. Along with Miss Alice Birkbeck and Miss E. Fernie, Miss Carter ran the town's second auxiliary war hospital at Wellingtonia, also on Mundesley Road. Opened on 25 January 1915, with 15 beds, throughout the war it admitted 475 patients. It closed on 21 January 1919.

Miss Grace Holloway, matron at the Lower House VAD Hospital 1915–19. Miss Holloway was one of the founder members of the Women's Voluntary Aid Detachment (Norfolk No. 80), British Red Cross Society in the town in 1914. After serving throughout the First World War she was appointed Commandant and reorganized the local branch in 1919.

The Sopwith Pup biplane is 'centre stage' in the Market Place for the opening of North Walsham's War Bond Week, 4 March 1918. Coupled with ubiquitous patriotism, parades and displays, the bonds raised over £27,000 for the war effort. They were sold from a specially erected hut situated opposite Barclays Bank and manned by Miss Gertrude Wilkinson and Arthur Coleman.

The town band, followed by the scouts, lead the procession as it rounds into Grammar School Road on its way to the Market Place for the main celebrations to honour 'Peace Day' on Saturday 19 July 1919.

North Walsham men who served in the First World War gather for a photograph in Ship Yard before their complimentary dinner in the Church Rooms on Friday 25 July 1919.

St John Ambulance and Air Raid Precautions Committee Annual General Meeting on the lawn at Eastgate on New Road, July 1938. Left to right: Walter Dack (Hon. Assistant Secretary), Dr Cecil Taylor, Mrs Taylor, Dr Cecil Herbert Winter Page (President), Frank Randell (Chairman of ARP) and George Burton Fuller (St John Divisional Superintendent). As the threat of war loomed large in the 1930s with the added danger of attacks on civilian targets from the air, Air Raid Precautions Committees were established in North Norfolk as early as 1936 to commence training volunteers in anti-gas and rescue.

'G.B.' Fuller, on the right and without gas mask, supervises the gas mask and rescue drill in 1937. Everyone else present is wearing the 'Service' respirator, issued to military personnel and heavy rescue parties.

Evacuees from Edmonton and Bethnal Green arriving in the Market Place on 1 September 1939. They represented a tiny fraction of the first evacuation from London, which amounted to a total of 827,000 schoolchildren, 524,000 mothers and children under school age, nearly 13,000 expectant mothers, 7,000 blind or otherwise handicapped people and 103,000 teachers and helpers.

Grouped together in front of their converted laundry truck ambulance at North Walsham in 1939 are the first mobile unit crews, many of them uniformed with only an arm band and a tin helmet, of the Norfolk County Council Casualty Services. Many of them were extant ambulance members. The regular ambulance was not used because the larger mobile unit was required, and indeed specially designed, to carry supplies, blankets and compressed cardboard coffins for the anticipated thousands of casualties during the blitz on our cities. Thank God so many were not needed.

Maj Gen MacHardy laying the foundation stone of the blast-proof ARP depot on New Road, 1940. The finished building was opened by Sir Bartle Frere in the autumn of that year. From that time, two casualty service men were on duty there every night. They were often accompanied by Civil Defence messenger boys, while two nurses slept at Mrs Ferrier's nearby ready to respond to any emergency.

Some of the officers of North Walsham and District Civil Defence Committee at the cattle market, c. 1942. They were responsible for training civilians in all manner of air raid precautions, from gas masks to extinguishing incendiary bombs with sand and stirrup pumps. At the time, typed notices were sent to local households instructing them what to do in an emergency. Among the directives sent to Ernest Vincent of Aylsham Road were: to hold emergency rations; to keep as many receptacles as possible filled with water, in case the town water supply failed; to have bandages ready, which could be made from any old linen. The instructions also point out that if you are not in possession of a shelter, you should dig a trench 4 ft 6 in by 2 ft 6 in wide to afford protection from bomb splinters!

Men of 'A' Company, 5th Battalion, Norfolk Home Guard in front of their HQ at the Paston Grammar School, c. 1943. Formed as Local Defence Volunteers after Anthony Eden, Secretary of State for War's radio appeal on 14 May 1940 for men too old, unfit or in War Reserved Occupations, the unit was under the overall command of Brig Gen W.A. Blake CMG, DSO.

Men of 'B' Company, 6th (34th GPO) Cambridgeshire Regiment, Home Guard, Cable Repeater Station, Mundesley Road, *c.* 1943. Back row, left to right: Jack Taylor, Mr Strapps (postmaster), Frank Mann, Charlie Larkins, George Oakley, Lenny Brown (Inspector of Engineers), 'Tubby' Cutting, Jimmy Duncan, Edgar Richardson (postman). Middle row: Cpl Bob Lancaster, Sgt Bertie Manning (survey officer), Cpl Edgar Cook (gang foreman). Front row: Cyril Chatten, Bertie Lawrence, Derek Manning.

A parade of local Home Guard units, *c.* 1943, marches up the Market Place led by Lord Ironside, who is accompanied by Maj Percival Pickford DSO, MC, North Walsham's Company Commander and headmaster of the Paston Grammar School. It must have made an impressive sight as the battalion numbered a total of 77 officers and 1,724 other ranks, with companies as far apart as Mundesley and Scottow.

North Walsham and District Special Constables after their inspection by the Chief Constable Capt Stephen Van Neck MC, *c.* 1943. With many policemen called up, the Specials stepped into the breach carrying out regular police duties and beat patrols. Often a thankless task, their job was not made any easier with the war situation as they were called on to check identity cards, watch for 'spivs', ensure gas masks were carried, track down missing evacuees, help maintain the blackout and check vehicle lights were correctly masked.

The final group photo after the stand down parade of the town's wartime civilian emergency services in 1945. The dismiss was given by Supt 'G.B.' Fuller, the Joint Ambulance Committee depot ambulance officer. The group consisted of WVS ladies, Civil Defence, St John Ambulance Men and St John Ambulance Women's Section. The latter group, described as 'A credit to the town and service to which they belonged', attended numerous plane crashes as well as serving on the motor ambulance during the blitz on Norwich. In recognition of their services, they earned the distinction of becoming the only county section where women were allowed to join a men's division after the war.

The dedication of the North Walsham 1939–45 Roll of Honour by the Bishop of Thetford, in the Parish Church of St Nicholas, May 1950. The memorial to the forty-five men of the town who died in the conflict was crafted by local master carver Len Roper, who is pictured to the right of the memorial in his capacity as 'People's Warden' to the church. The service, conducted by Revd R.H. Bradshaw, was concluded by the sounding of the Last Post and the laying of wreaths.

The links between townspeople and the Norfolk Cyclists stationed there during the First World War were strong and happy; indeed for many years (until there were too few alive to make it worthwhile) there was an annual reunion dinner of 6th Cyclists at The King's Arms, followed by a band-led torchlight parade. To preserve these links for posterity, there is a plaque to the 6th Cyclists in the church in addition to the magnificent memorial plaque to their commanding officer, Col Bernard Henry Leathes Prior DSO, TD. He is seen here when the plaque was unveiled by the Bishop of Norwich on 1 May 1955 are, left to right: Maj M.W.L. Prior, Col B.O.L. Prior, the Lord Bishop of Norwich, and Capt Wallace M. Palmer.

CHAPTER EIGHT

THE DISTRICT

Cubitt & Son's delivery cart, c. 1905, on its rounds delivering all manner of tinned foods, cheese, millinery and general goods to the surrounding settlements within an 8 mile radius of North Walsham.

Wayford Bridge Hotel, Smallburgh, *c.* 1904. A trading post on the River Ant since ancient times, Wayford's importance was enhanced by the cutting of the North Walsham and Dilham Canal in the 1820s. As the wharf developed, handling coal and flour, a maltings was also erected along with a beerhouse, kept by Robert Saul in the 1840s. Enlarged and improved by Charles Couzens at the turn of the century, it became the Wayford Bridge Hotel, once familiar to many Broads visitors.

An evocative broadland study of a wherry and moored pleasure craft on the River Ant at Wayford, *c.* 1910. Once on the canal wherries paid their dues per mile and were thus connected to the many mills that existed along the navigation to Antingham Ponds. In 1844 fees ranged from, for example, 3d. on coal, 3d. on corn and flour, ¹⁄₂d. on manure or marl and ¹⁄₂d. on goods.

A charming study of St Peter's Church, Smallburgh, *c.* 1908. The original tower fell in 1677 and considerable restorations were carried out in the nineteenth century. A new bell cote for two bells was built under the supervision of Mr W.I. Tapper, architect, at a total cost of £1,765, which included one recast bell presented by Revd F. Jickling MA, JP.

Smallburgh Rectory, *c.* 1904. The Rectory was given as a gift by the Bishop of Norwich in the nineteenth century. At the time it was photographed, the living was held by Revd James Russell MA and had a net yearly value of £250, including 28 acres of glebe land.

Thatched corner cottages off Smallburgh Hill, *c.* 1903. When this photograph was taken the population of Smallburgh stood at 444, the number boosted by the inclusion of the 73 officers and inmates of the Tunstead and Happing Workhouse.

Dilham Street, 1904. To the left is the Primitive Methodist Chapel and schoolroom, built in 1869 at a total cost of £150. The village, scattered over 1,563 acres, was home to 426 inhabitants at the turn of the century.

Local boys having a splash about are watched by their friends on the bank in this nostalgic study of Dilham Green and stream, *c.* 1910. H. Morse-Taylor inhabited The Rookery. Once a 'watery morass over 25 acres', he converted it to 'one of the prettiest pleasure grounds in the county', consisting of six landscaped islands connected by ornamental bridges. It was so beautiful that The Rookery was renamed The Islands.

Dilham Staithe Windmill, *c.* 1905, was built by Robert Mason in the early nineteenth century as a flour mill. Its longest-serving incumbent was George Doughty, between 1883 and 1926, who combined his milling with the job of local 'Assessor and Collector of Income Tax'. The mill had become derelict in the 1930s and was demolished.

Dilham Watermill, pictured in about 1905, was built in the early nineteenth century. When the canal was being constructed the problems of water flow had to be considered, so a dam of 25 acres was formed in 1828. The mill was operational until the early twentieth century, when its last miller, Mr Sidney Stackwood, moved on to Bacton Wood Mill. The mill's machinery was salvaged for the war effort during the First World War. Today, there is hardly anything left to show there was ever a mill on the site.

St Nicholas' Church, Dilham, c. 1908. Four or five churches of varying grandeur have stood on this site over the years. The first, built by William de Glanville in about 1125, was replaced by an impressive edifice constructed by Sir Roger Gyney. It had a particularly fine tower that became sadly dilapidated and was demolished and rebuilt in 1836. When it fell down again in 1900 the stone was reused to build a bapistry. The church pictured here was demolished in 1930, replaced by yet another in 1931 built by the local ecclesiastical carvers Cornish & Gaymer.

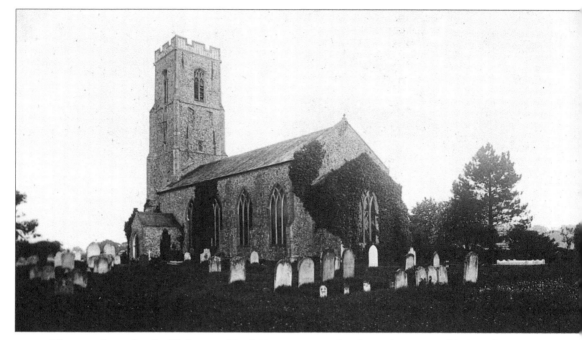

The magnificent church of St Peter and Paul, Honing, pictured in about 1910. It is visible for miles around, placed as it is on its high mound. It was rebuilt in 1795 with the exception of the tower and the arcades of the nave, which were built up and the aisles repaired. A notable length of service was achieved by Revd John Alfred Laurence, who faithfully served as Rector of Honing from 1872 until his death in 1930.

A wonderful collection of locals and watermen in their 'bests'; hats are certainly the order of the day for ladies as they gather for this wedding group photograph at Honing, c. 1910.

Honing Street, *c.* 1912. All set behind fine white picket fences, on the left is the post office, run at this time by sub-postmistress Mrs Anne Riches. Beyond that is the Temperance Hall, which became the men's club after the First World War and was the venue for popular smoking concerts and local entertainments for many years.

Mrs Tricker the mistress, with one of her young teachers, keeps a watchful eye over the children posing for the camera at Honing School, *c.* 1910. The Mixed Public Elementary School was erected in 1871; it was enlarged in 1892 and again in 1903 to accommodate eighty-two children.

The place-name of Honing is derived from the Old English *Haninga* – meaning 'the people at the hill' – so it is apt to view some of its extent with this unusual postcard taken from the high ground on Station Road hill in about 1912. To the right, among the trees, is the M&GN station; to the left is Briggate Mill; further still, on the skyline to the left, we may view the mighty tower of St Mary's Church in Worstead.

M&GN Railway, Honing station, *c.* 1910. Increasing demand resulted in the construction of a half-mile passing loop brought into use in 1901 to ease and control the flow of traffic, especially during busy holiday periods. Fred Davey, the Honing East signalman, proudly claimed he once put eighty-four trains through Honing station in twenty-four hours. Today just the platforms are left, and the old station area has become a car park for the pleasant walk known as Weavers Way, which now runs along much of the old track line.

The Yarmouth Beach and Midlands express in full steam passing Honing, *c.* 1935. Such trains would run frequently along the lines near the village in the summer time, providing great entertainment for the children, who would line the fences and gates along the route to watch them pass.

The Yarmouth Beach to Southampton fish train passing under Honing railway bridge, *c.* 1935. Along this route and on to the Honing sidings trains were known to proceed unofficially slowly to enable the engine's fireman to bag some of the many rabbits that were caught in the gin traps set by Tim Watts on the banks.

The dedication of East Ruston's War Memorial, *c.* 1922. Revd Herbert Gladstone Pickard, Rector of East Ruston and Ridington, leads the service, joined by the choir and watched by many locals and dignitaries. The memorial, paid for entirely by public subscription, was erected to the memory of the nineteen men of the village who fell during the First World War.

Hold you on steady bor'! Billy Walpole, the apprentice boy, steadies the pony while the expert hands of Arthur Plummer, third generation blacksmith of East Ruston, files down the hoof at the old smithy on Stalham Road, *c.* 1925.

Crostwight Manor House, *c.* 1904. The house was built in the mid-sixteenth century by John and Miles Le Groos (or Gross), the first men to own the entire Manor of Crostweyt. It remained in their family until the 1720s when it was sold to Robert Walpole, later Earl of Orford, the first statesman to be recognized as Britain's Prime Minister. He later went on to build Houghton Hall, the biggest county house in Norfolk. The ancient manor house had a lesser fate; replaced by a later and enlarged hall it was in a state of ruin by the late nineteenth century.

Witton Bridge post office, *c.* 1900, when the sub-postmaster, grocer and draper was Charles Cole. The village is considered to be one of the longest and most scattered in North Norfolk: its residents live in an area that stretches from just outside North Walsham almost to the coast.

Ebridge Mill, *c.* 1904. A water-mill has been on this site since Domesday. The scene of so much history, one of its finest hours must have been when the official celebrations for the opening of the North Walsham & Dilham Canal culminated here. The mill has now been in the hands of Cubitt & Walker for generations, their operation incorporating wind-, water- and steam-mills at Ebridge, White Horse Common, Worstead, Stalham and Swafield at the turn of the century. By the 1920s they concentrated on Ebridge and Briggate Mills, both on the canal. Cubitt & Walker ran their own wherrys and eventually purchased the canal itself in 1921 for £1,500. Although they sold the canal, Ebridge Mill is still in family hands, producing quality animal feeds.

The Congregational Chapel, Bradfield, *c.* 1912. This commodious building replaced a thatched barn where the Independents/Congregationalists were forced to meet from the 1650s until the 1689 Toleration Act, which permitted the erection of buildings specifically for non-conformist worship. The new purpose-built chapel was opened in 1872 at a cost of £500, and could accommodate 170 worshippers.

St Margaret's was once the church for the Manor of St Bennet, which abutted the enclosure, but existed in its own right. In the Domesday survey it is recorded as over 8 furlongs long and 5¹⁄₂ broad, and that it paid 13¹⁄₂d. in gelt. After the dissolution of the monasteries, St Bennet's was bought privately and gradually amalgamated with Antingham. Although it had rectors into the eighteenth century, St Margaret's had fallen into such disrepair that materials from it were used to repair St Mary's in 1702 and again in 1764. All that is left today is the gaunt tower, seemingly held together by the ivy that now covers it.

Homeward bound after a hard day in the fields, Alfred Hammond, the team-man on Gunton Park Farm, and young Rosemary Parfitt pause for the camera, c. 1950. This scene, once so common, was fading fast as automation on the farm became affordable and available after the Second World War.

Felmingham Watermill, *c.* 1905. Situated on a tributary of the Bure, a mill has existed on the site for over 200 years and is shown beside a windmill on Faden's Map of 1797. Kept at the turn of the nineteenth century by Thomas Gaze, the farmer and miller, it passed into the hands of the well-known local millers Barclay, Pallett & Co. Ltd in the early '20s. They had depots in town and at GER stations at North Walsham, Bacton Wood Staithe, Cromer, Gunton, Wayford Bridge, Cawston, Aylesham and Wroxham. The mill produced and distributed cattle cake, corn, coal, seed, hay, straw and manure.

Swanton Abbot Hall, *c.* 1905. The original house at the rear dates back to the sixteenth century, and was the seat of the Blake family for generations, many of whose memorials appear in the local church. The Tudor chimneys and crow step gables were retained when the new frontage to the house was added in 1858.

A fine study of Lion Corner, Buxton, *c.* 1900. The two local postmen lean by the wall in the foreground; behind them, beside the carriage, is the village post office kept at the time by Walter Woods, who also acted as grocer and butcher. The carriage is probably that of William Gostling, the local carrier, who passed through the Waggon and Horses on Wednesdays and Saturdays, returning the same evening.

Mill Street, Buxton, *c.* 1900. The rutted and lined surface of the roadway belies an earlier time of unmetalled surfaces when roads were made of Wymondham flints covered with binding silt, and carriages, carts and even the occasional motor car would throw up great clouds of dust as they passed through. In the summer time the water cart and spray bar would be a welcome sight on its rural rounds to 'lay the dust'.

Buxton Mill, *c.* 1904, was built in 1754 on the banks of the Bure. The trading waterway was greatly improved by the installation of locks (visible to the far left) in the 1770s, used regularly by the mighty trading wherries that carried the corn and milled flour to and from the mill. The mill itself was run in the mid-nineteenth century by Cooke and Gambling, corn millers and merchants; for the latter half of the century it was taken over by Thomas Shreeve, the miller, coal and general dealer, who sold it on to Ling & Co., the corn millers, coal, cake, seed and salt merchants. Run in the 1920s by J. Parker and Sons, and in the 1930s by William Charles Duffield, the old mill has been resurrected after a major fire in 1991 to become business premises and a restaurant.

Buxton School, *c.* 1905. The original school was established in 1833 under the will of John Wright, 'for the good of the poor children of Buxton and adjoining parishes', and was greatly enlarged in 1855 by Canon Anson. Catering for all the children of the parish, the National School (Infants) was run at the turn of the century by Miss May Kidd, and the British School for the older children by John Capper.

Buxton Vicarage, *c.* 1910. It was built by Revd William James Stracey MA, rector 1855–89, and required a staff of at least twelve servants. In 1936 a new vicarage was built under the direction of the then rector, Revd Herbert Walker Benson MA, at a total cost of £2,450, and the old living was renamed Levishaw Manor.

John Colman at the head and William Digby at the handles of the horse-drawn lawn mower at Buxton Vicarage, *c.* 1910. Mr Digby followed in his father James' footsteps to become the village sexton. In James' day he was specifically not termed 'Parish Clerk' and by some ancient charge had to rent his land from the Crown for £4 per annum (the rent was returned to him by the parish). He was also required by deed to deliver up the keys of the sexton's cottage at the Vestry Meeting each year.

The Anchor of Hope, Lammas, *c.* 1908. This ancient river-side alehouse was kept by a number of landlords over the years. One of the most notable was Arthur Edward Sexton, who ran the hostelry in the early years of the twentieth century. Beginning as a saddler and harness-maker, a trade he continued in an adjoining shed when he took over the pub, he also responded to the growing interest from Broadland visitors by hiring out day and fishing boats as well as a pony and trap to explore the area.

Taken from the Anchor of Hope when one of its boats had to be used as a temporary ferry after the bridge was swept away 'with a tide-like force', during the great flood of Monday 26 August 1912.

Christmas came a few days early in Scottow in years past when Santa, accompanied by 'helpers' from RAF Coltishall, visited the older local residents to deliver cheer and presents. Here 74-year-old Mrs Elizabeth Cutting of the Fairstead is presented with her gifts. Her house was never fitted with electricity, an inside toilet or piped water. Until well into her 80s she would walk over 150 yards down the road to the village pump to get a bucket of water.

Nice to see a few smiles, although some children still look unsure of the camera as they gather for the group portrait at Scottow Parochial School, *c.* 1900. The school was erected in 1859, on land given by Sir H.T. Estridge Durrant Bart. of Scottow Hall. Built for ninety children, the average attendance in 1900 was fifty-one. The mistress was Miss Pattison.

The old Three Horse Shoes public house at Scottow, *c.* 1912. Known in the local dialect as the 'Scutta Hu'shoos' it was kept at the time by William James Tooke, first in a long line of Tooke family members to keep the pub over the years. Until the late nineteenth century an annual cattle and horse fair was held in and around the inn on Easter Tuesday.

Four Scottow characters line up by the Three Horse Shoes, *c.* 1935. Left to right: Alan Took, 'Tiddler' Newstead, Billy Pardon, Roger Took (keeper of the Horse Shoes). 'Tiddler' was known in all the villages around North Walsham for many years as he and his father would trot around the district selling firewood from a cart pulled by a piebald horse.

Superintendent James Craske of the North Walsham Fire Brigade (in his brass fire helmet) surveys the damage to a burnt out petrol truck near Sloley, *c.* 1930. Other members of the brigade, all volunteers summoned from their places of work, hence the various degrees of uniform, attended the scene 'in full cry'. Having brought the blaze under control, they have removed their helmets and some have replaced their civilian hats. They are now clearing the scene, and shovelling road silt to absorb the spilt petrol.

Station Road, Worstead, *c.* 1912. The road, familiar to many a weary traveller, leads to Worstead station, which is in fact about 1 mile away in Sloley. In early May of every year the fields and roads around here would be filled with cattle and horses for the annual fair held on the Fairstead until the late nineteenth century. Today the fields are still thronged every July by visitors from all over the country coming to the Worstead Festival. It began in 1966 and is still going strong!

Harry Yaxley, the Worstead blacksmith, 1938. When a boy, Harry served a short apprenticeship with a blacksmith but thought he would prefer farm work so he left. However, the lure of the forge was too great and he returned and sharpened his trade skills as a shoeing smith in the army during the First World War, serving most of his time in the Salonika campaigns. After discharge he worked at the Scottow forge for seven years before opening his own business in Worstead.

Church Plain, Worstead, *c.* 1903. On the right was the old bakery, kept for many years by Samuel Grimes. Beyond that, the fine Flemish gables hark back to the days of the Flemish weavers who made the village into the town that it was all those years ago. One of the ancient village benefactor families was the Tucks. One of them, Raphael, was born in the village and went on to found the nationally renowned *Tuck's Almanac.*

Looking down Church Plain from the Manor House, *c.* 1904. Worstead was once a town of some importance with houses spreading out to its outlying hamlets of Holgate, Withergate, Bengate, Briggate, Lyngate, Brockley and Meeting House Hill. In very early times the town's market was held here every Saturday; it was moved to North Walsham after plague broke out in the village in 1666.

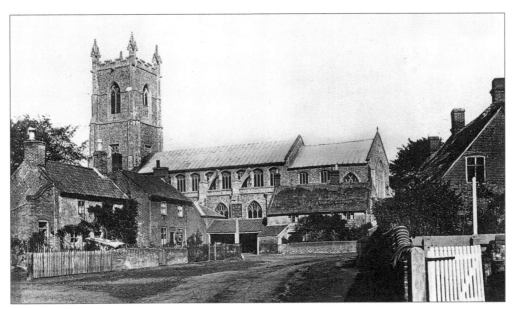

St Mary's Church and the New Inn, Front Street, Worstead, *c.* 1910. Once another pub, the King's Head, stood nearby. James Swan Burrell, the local carrier and mole catcher, was a familiar sight at the turn of the century, trotting up this roadway to pick up wares from in front of the pubs in his carrier's cart every Tuesday and Friday for his run to Norwich.

St Mary's Church and the New Inn, Worstead, *c.* 1908. The embattled 109 ft tower is capped by scaffolding with a movable gantry for its restoration in 1908 (for the grand sum of £800), following a programme of general repairs at the turn of the century. The tower contains six bells, varying in weight from 5 cwt to 1 ton, all cast at the Norwich bell foundry between 1635 and 1723. The tower also boasts a clock, purchased for £62 in 1770. The Victorian pinnacles were removed in the 1960s following lightning damage.

Arthur W. Colthorpe (far left), later headmaster of North Walsham Board School, stands proudly as master beside his pupils at Worstead Public Elementary School, *c.* 1910. The schoolhouse was opened in 1844, funded by subscription and supplemented by a grant of £365 for 60 boys and 40 girls. Most of the students paid 2d. a week or, if their parents could afford it, 5s. a quarter.

Boys of the 2nd Worstead Troop, Boy Scouts, accompanied by the gamekeeper, at Worstead Hall lake, *c.* 1928. I dare say the old gamekeeper was not so happy when some of the boys accompanied their fathers 'rabbiting' or poaching a couple of pheasants in the twilight hours.

Boys from the Meeting Hill Baptist Church Sunday school, *c.* 1922. Back row, left to right: Jimmy Adams, Reggie Hales. Front row, seated: Jack Amiss, Percy Steward, George Kirk, John Self, Frank Cutting and Arthur Bullimore.

The old toll-bar cottage, Westwick, *c.* 1904. Constructed to collect the tolls on the Norwich to North Walsham Turnpike, the cottages were built complete with gates, wells and 'necessary houses' in 1797 by Jeremiah Huson, bricklayer, of North Walsham and William Gill, carpenter, of Aylsham for £123. With each house came 30 perches of land. The first collector of tolls at North Walsham was Cornelius Culley. He received a wage of £20 a year on the terms that he ' . . . do attend at the said gate every morning at 5 o'clock and not leave the same until 9 at night'.

Westwick Hall and lake, *c.* 1904. Built in about 1710 by John Berney Esq., the house stands on the northern slope of a picturesque valley that stretches down to the margin of a rivulet that is expanded into a lake of 30 acres from which an aqueduct was cut to another lake near the house. John Berney Petre further improved the estate with a carriage drive of 5 miles through a plantation of 500 acres, for which he received a medal from the Society of Arts.

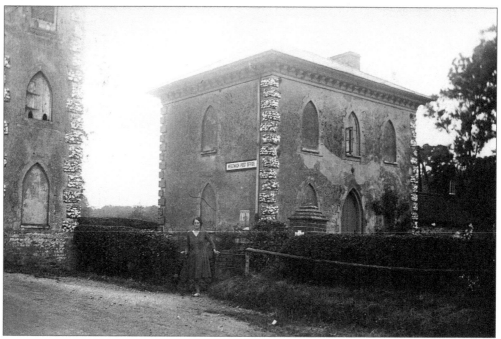

Westwick post office, *c.* 1927. The sub-postmaster and small general stores was run by William 'Tuffun' Watling. To send telegraphs, however, residents had to travel 3 miles to the post office at North Walsham.

Westwick Arch, *c.* 1911. Built in about 1780, the arch marked the entrance to the Berney Petre estate and was used as a grand dovecote. John Berney Petre, Lord of the Manor and principal landowner of Westwick, was one of the original trustees on the North Walsham Rota of the Norwich to North Walsham turnpike and was happy to have the profitable diversion of the road to skirt his estate through the arch, which then straddled the road. The lodges were built either side, one of which later became the post office. In 1799 the trustees decided to let the turnpike tolls by auction. The Crostwick Gate was let for £90 and North Walsham for £80. By 1820 traffic had increased so much that when the leases were renewed they had increased to £260 and £121 respectively. With the coming of the railways, turnpikes met their demise by the end of the nineteenth century. The road was adopted by the council under the schemes of the 1890s and traffic continued to flow. The arch remained a familiar feature until it was demolished to much public outcry in September 1981.

ACKNOWLEDGEMENTS

The author gratefully acknowledges the following, without whom this book would not have been possible:

Philip Standley, Basil Gowen, Mike Ling, Kay Bowman Phyl Scott, Lindsey and Don at the Beechwood Hotel, Ivor Self, Freddy 'Applejack' Gibbons, Joan Anholt, Jill Allen, Stanley Lowe, Dick Waters, Richard Hunter at Paston Sixth Form College, Jimmy Adams, Frederick Mace ARPS, Ken and Nick Allen, the M&GN Circle, Norwich Central Library Local Studies Department, the Salvation Army International Heritage Centre.

Thanks yet again to Terry Burchell for the usual photographic wonders and to my Dad for the computerized restoration of the badly creased and damaged photo of Smallburgh Workhouse.

I give an especial thanks in this my tenth year of published writing to all those who have encouraged or inspired me, supported each of my publications (it is a strange, humbling and honoured feeling to be a collected author) and to those who have so generously donated photographs, documents or memories to my collection over the years.

I give heartfelt thanks to all my family, old, new and those I have known and loved but who are now sadly in the great mardlin' house in the sky. Finally, but by no means least, I wish to record my love and appreciation for my wife Sarah and all the things she does for this temperamental author.

Every attempt has been made to obtain permission from copyright holders to reproduce photographs and acknowledge them. However, because of the age and anonymity of some of the photographers, it has not always been possible. Please accept my apologies; no breach of those rights was intended.

Everyone having a great time on the outing from the Black Swan, *c.* 1948 – Cheers!